FALLING WALLENDAS

MICHAEL R. BROWN

TIA CHUCHA PRESS, CHICAGO

The following poems have been previously published:

"Angels," "Bookshelves," *Kameleon* (1992, 1990); "Autumn," "Bearer Donates Body to Nature," *Galley Sail* (1990, 1992); "The Book Cliffs," *Red Tree 3* (1991); "Forget to Remember," *Red Brick Review* (1994); "The Ice Worm," *Wail!* (1992); "In the Good Old Summer," "Statues in the Park," *Amandla Ngewethu!* (1991); "Jody and the Tigers," *Kudzu* (1979); "Making Love to Death," *Nashville's Poetry Newsletter* (1992); "Poiseidon at the Point Diner," *Venture II* (1992); "The Potter's Mistress," *Another Chicago Magazine IV* (1979); "Reflection," *Menagerie* (1984); "Thoreau's Last Words," *Greenfield Review* (1975); "Tompkins Square Park," *Stone Soup Poetry Gazette* (1991).

Four lines in "Teaching" are quoted from "Renascence" by Edna St. Vincent Millay, *Collected Poems* (New York: Harper & Row, 1956), p.13.

COVER PHOTOS: (top) Bob Kalmbach, Courtesy University of Michigan, (middle and bottom) Marc Harris.

BOOK DESIGN: Jane Brunette Kremsreiter

Printed in the United States.

ISBN 1-882688-02-3

Library of Congress Catalog Card Number: 94-76369

TIA CHUCHA PRESS
A Project of The Guild Complex
PO Box 476969
Chicago IL 60647
312-252-5321
Fax: 312-252-5388

This project is partially supported by grants from the National Endowment for the Arts, the Illinois Arts Council, and the City of Chicago Department of Cultural Affairs. Special thanks to the Lannan Foundation for a grant to publicize this and other Tia Chucha Press projects.

For the positive political and cultural aspects of my development I wish to thank a number of adversaries too great to be counted and a few long-standing supportive friends— James Beloungy, Peter Bowen, Ron Foreman, Harriet (Happy) Green, J. Kovar, Linda Mastaglio, Jennifer Pickering, Diana Seifert, Dan Swanson, and my wife, Patricia Smith.

The specific content of this book is dedicated to three personal heroes, The Falling Wallendas, Eddie Balchowsky, Sydney Harris and Robert Hayden "...he was bareback rider of them all."

CONTENTS

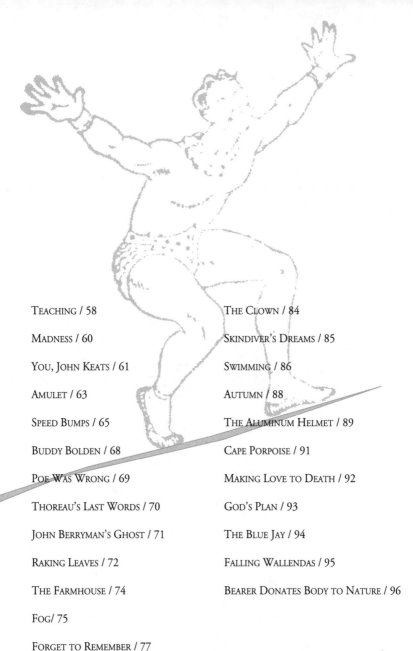

THE ICE WORM

You can take away that net.
  I'm not much of a performer,
   one of those that struts and shines,
  delivering my personal angst
 in easy technicolor rhymes.
I'm from the old school
where poets named things, told the truth—
the hard truths nobody wanted to hear.
When they created beauty,
by God, people were stunned.
When they failed,
they took the fall.

Truth, beauty, the arcane lore,
what are they against *People* magazine,
USA Today, CNN, and a lying president?
Mass production, the glory and curse of the 20th century,
replays words, pictures, politics and bad art
until it all seeps in like an Eskimo winter,
and sometimes the only way to clear the synapses
is a vigorous cranial wallbanger—or a good poem.
So let me tell you something I remember.
Maybe you've seen it, too.

At four or five years old,
when I was starting to lose my imagination,
had stopped coloring dogs' tongues orange and cats' feet purple,
I must have been home from school sick
and bored with staying inside the lines,
when I saw something where nothing should have been.

Atop a bare sycamore branch
where the sun should have melted it away,

a piece of ice moved.
It humped itself up like an inchworm
and moved along,
humped and moved,
humped and moved.
When it got to the end of the branch,
its head searched and couldn't find anywhere to go,
so it humped off the end of the branch and fell
with a couple of tumbling flashes into a snowbank below.

Once I saw one, I saw more.
They were on the trees, the snow and the sidewalks.
As my chest and throat and head
were about to burst with excitement,
my mother came up behind me.
She saw what I saw,
and light flashed in her warm brown eyes
the way it had off the ice worm.
She opened the window and slid her finger
under one on the window sill.
I watched it inch along.
Before it got to the end,
I picked it up,
and all I felt was dampness
between my thumb and forefinger.

I haven't seen an ice worm in years.
I'm not sure what that means, except for this—
there ought to be things that we can't see easily,
that TV networks, magazines, companies,
and the goddamned politicians can't use,
small, beautiful things that disappear
as soon as we get our hands on them.

CHORUS

This mellow sense of longing feels like a muted trumpet solo
    late at night;
  golden notes on an ornamental chain wound round a sinuous
    African waist;
 Miles' eyes gleaming brighter than his horn,
bleating tortured soul, intelligent love,
his dexterity a dance,
a string of fiery arabesques tracing sad feelings of a song too soon gone.

Long after the circus has bedded down for the night on silk golden straw,
the tightrope walker returns to the tent.
A long blue note eases out from the platform,
slides a toe on the wire and rubs it back and forth,
resinous squeak vibrating the line on which his melody will advance.

A tentative cluster edges ahead on a weighty dare,
a chance,
a change,
an invitation to himself to step on air as vibrant as the wire,
holding up the complete loss of gravity except for one point
where human need,
pain,
and foolish emotion
replay in remembrance of weightlessness,
make him dance,
wow on the wire above the pale floor.

At midline he jumps, slides, flips
and turns exuberant painful figures in the air,
each move a tightly wrapped convolution
twirled in dark space like a Christmas ornament,
colorful recreation suspended and turning
giving back bright flash from a dark soul.

All of it spins around the inner ear,
that gyroscope of balance and harmony,
indispensible rightness of sure step and true note.

The ear;
airmaster,
place-fixer,
music conductor,
holding the center of this muted nighttime Wallenda
doing impossible tricks of his own device
to cure his soul of the pain of longing,
subject the immutable laws to his play,
just to make it to the other end of the wire,
slide down the rope,
walk out of the tent,
catch the dawn,
and never repeat the chorus in exactly the same way.

POSEIDON AT THE POINT DINER

His face looked like an old part of the expressway,
  worn to rolling pockmarked flatness;
   his eyes were seams in the asphalt.
  A tangle of old nets and seaweed,
 his hair tumbled down to his shoulders.
His voice was soft and deep,
the edge of a wave on a gravelly shore.
When he caught my stare, an undulation widened his eyes,
and in there I saw a cannon sun in a coppery sky
firing blazing pinwheels to a red horizon.
The sea boiled sailors' blood
and cooked ships' boards to a splintery stew.
Finger bones groped for freedom from the Sargasso Sea,
Ahab's obsession rendered to coral edges on oily knuckles.

This modern Poseidon knows huge ships with tiny crews
wreaking havoc all out of scale to the sea's revenge.
A hundred and fifty years ago we sent sailors
to drain the oceans of whales and light the Industrial Revolution.
Nowadays when a corporate leviathan loses its way
or splits an aging seam, we don't lose sailors' lives,
but living gets harder for all of us.
Seas and shores suffocate under thick film.
It's something sailors can't handle and companies can't fix;
oil and water, man and the sea, we still don't mix.

THE PEREGRINE FALCON

FOR JOE ROARTY

He was a tough little son of a bitch.
   I could see that by the way he stuck like a bullet
      in the dead branch of the catalpa across the street.
   Like a short wiry guy on Milwaukee Avenue
   with a razor in his pocket and a .22 at home
 in the bureau drawer, this sharp-beaked
spear-winged falcon took the block in at a glance.
Was there a victim here? Some absent-minded
city pigeon strutting without checking his back?

On the tidal flats of Delaware Bay ospreys
build huge mare's nests on phone poles.
Red-tailed hawks sit at the edges of farm fields
in the Midwest and keep highways clean.
In the far west golden eagles patrol the skies
and pick the mountain carrion.
We've brought them back by cutting down
on pesticides—a fair trade:
spots on apples, birds in the trees.

But this peculiar introduction of a high-velocity
killer into downtown canyons is a different bit of business.
It's one Chicago tradition, I suppose.
We import diminutive hit men to nail cripples,
shoot the weak, terrorize the vulnerable.

But it's also a bird for Republican times,
nesting in the lofty crags of banks,
out of reach of the common hand,
a swift small-caliber shooter that
kills those most deserving of our mercy.

It's that manipulation of the environment
they reach back to Darwin for
then muster righteous power and invade
vacation islands, desert kingdoms.
Natural resources that bring a quiet beauty
to our lives they sacrifice
to the flash of transient assassins,
the corporate field rep,
the advance man for fascism.

TOMPKINS SQUARE PARK

"DOUBT IS A CHASM FILLED WITH THE BONES OF LOST MAGIC."
—MICHAEL LIPUMA

A narrow ravine runs through the center of a Rangoon Park.
Outside, threading their way among wary Burmese
in sarongs and sports shirts,
teams of government men in trench coats and snap brim hats
arrest anyone who comes too close to Freedom Park.
In China the barren ground of hope is Tienanmen Square.

In America the chasm of lost magic is Tompkins Square Park.
Its chairs and wrought iron gone,
the police have tossed its homeless out into New York City.
A communist can sit and talk business in the 7A Cafe
while behind chain link fence I hear mumuring ghosts
who brush their teeth with their forefingers,
comb their greasy hair with their hands,
and sleep in cloth crates and plastic tents.

One takes out a complaint, sips the wild rose,
and passes the pint of resentment, the hard times
of hope shining out of the paper bag of friendship
until they hide their hunger and dignity under dirty tarpaulins.

They believed the president, voted for his regime
when they hurt, and now sit with embarrassed smiles
while the man from the *People's Tribune* orders more coffee
and no Preacher Casey calls up any lost magic.

No Richard Wright watches; no Steinbeck takes notes;
no Robeson or Guthrie aims rhetoric; no Dorothea Lange
points a camera; and no Emma Goldman harangues them
about how they must seize their country in their own hands.

Fed too long on bad principles
and abandoned by the champions of the underdog,
the homeless have lost their work, their voices, their names—
everything but their shame.
It's not enough to know with Gandhi that dictators always fall.
We must take back the land, control the police,
and give the tyrants a shove.

STATUES IN THE PARK

The little man swung his legs out of bed
   in the Lincoln Hotel and was surprised again
   by how rough worn down things could be—
   the hard edges of rickety furniture, prickly ends
   of old carpet, molding rounded by too much paint.
 Downstairs he ordered two coffees to go,
one with double cream and sugar. He said hello
to the man who drove in from Skokie to park
his Mercedes on the sidewalk and run the drugstore.

The little man walked across Clark Street, dodging
big cars and the Broadway bus. He steered his way
among patches of snow on the ball field south of the farm
in the zoo to where the dark clump lay by a tree, sheltered
from lake wind by a short row of upright shopping bags.

The little man called softly, but the lump didn't stir.
He set his coffee down and nudged gently at where
he guessed a shoulder to be. Gently he peeled back
the layer of tough plastic. He walked around to
the lake side and reached over a grocery bag to pull
at the stiff folds of a rancid sleeping bag. Just
below the dark knit cap two big brown lifeless eyes
stared through him. The lips were blue and green.
Mucous was frozen on the scruffy mustache. The little
man looked until his own awkwardly bent posture
stiffened. He shifted, then bent and put the coffee
with the extra next to his dead friend's head.

All winter long the little man had brought coffee
to the man who slept in the park. He gave the rich
cup to the dark man who did not thank him. The little
man pried the plastic cap from the styrofoam. The

16

homeless man coughed and spat as he unwrapped
himself. He'd piss nonchalantly behind a tree,
the coffee offering held at shoulder height. He busied
himself rearranging bags, bits of clothes, packing up.
He never talked, but he wouldn't move along until the
little man finished his coffee and walked away.

This morning the little man didn't walk away.
He had thought of the man in the park as a relative
in a distant town, someone to visit, but not to worry about
as long as he was on his own. Now they seemed closer.

Beyond the clump a wisp of steam rose off the coffee
next to the dead man. Cars whizzed along Lake Shore Drive.
The longer he was held there by the lump on the ground,
the more the little man hated those indifferent ones who drove
to work or to shop. "Stop!" he wanted to scream. "Look!
My friend is dead." Yet as the rage rose, he saw how
dead we all are. This little man living in a cheap hotel
had made one connection to another person, and he
wanted everyone to take notice. If they had been alive
at all, his friend would still be breathing, too.

If we buy sleek metal tubes to carry us from cozy homes
to stuffy offices, we can expect to die in such places.
Even if we escape those treadmills, the ways of our lives
will lead us to nursing homes, oxygen tents, machinery
to keep us going in ways we are accustomed to.
The little man realized he had come here every day
to honor a man he did not know, but who chose
to live in the fresh air, free, on this open ground
between tall buildings and a crowded roadway next to
a jail for animals. We die where we choose to live.
We go in the ways we know—a passionate political
leader at his desk in city hall, a ballplayer on the court,
a tightrope walker falling on the edge of the ring.

So the little man could see his end in the bright morning,
crumpled next to a cup of coffee brought as homage
to a friend he never knew yet believed in completely.
The little rebukes of both of them were small tributes
to those who make themselves monuments, reminders,
statues in the park.

TWILIGHT IN THE MARKETPLACE

In D.C. we see three to a street
   laid out like fat doormats in inconspicuous colors
    next to shops, on warm air grates
just below street level on avenues named for the states.

Chicago has an abandoned person in every block.
Seattle crowds them into the original skid row.
In Minneapolis they huddle in the snow
because they have no place else to go.

In afternoon sunlight ladies sit on high house steps,
coats wound around scabby legs, cigarets
and coffee cup in one hand until shelter doors
open at day's end and they can shuffle in.
Men gather in pocket parks and gab
or huddle alone on wooden benches,
wrapped in stale sour smells no one mentions.

They resent the world and will not leave it.
They would live in it if they could.
In better days Aztecs scattered corn
along the highways for travelers to eat.
We make our human sacrifices one meal at a time.

When people put on uniforms,
they lose some individuality
but gain substantial presence;
we know when a suit is in the room.
But it's easy to ignore the homeless
who make feeble calls for money, food, a cigaret,
and don't ask for what they really need.

Nelson Mandela,
    kept alive in the minds of others for 27 years,
Leonard Peletier,
    breathing with the aid of others' abstract sense of justice,
Aung Sun Suu Kyi,
    a tiny flame in a dark place.
    The fading light at the end of her night is us.
Wang Xizhe,
    out of prison after 14 years because he obeyed the rules
    and everybody forgot who he was.
In a population of one billion divided by one billion,
he has become the perfect collective unit,
the number of a fearful, silent conscience,
tightroping alone at twilight in the marketplace
because he cannot stand in Tienanmen Square,
he cannot approach Freedom Park.
Among millions of people who do not know him,
he fades into dusk that marks the end of day.

ABSALOM, ABSALOM

Northwest wind rattles the shutters;
  snow cushions street sounds
    while trees creak and clatter outside a window caked with ice.
  I always associate this scene with Faulkner's novel
   and think of my son living most of his life like me,
in cheap apartments atop three flights of wooden stairs—
isolate, creative, longing for a few things
the world will never give him.
Some of us are born for sacrifice,
and even if our fathers would be kings,
they cannot stop it.
                    Oh, Absalom, my son.
That would have been your name
if I had had my way. Or Abraham.
Which the greater pain, to be the son
who his father cannot save
or the father slitting the son's throat?

I made tentative steps toward the soldier's way
to visit my anger in vengeful Armageddon on the world,
then pulled back before the awful realities of such masquerades.
I never woke on Ash Wednesday with limbs and torsos
of honest folk piled in bloody array around me,
my motley costume singed, mud-caked,
felt my wide eyes invaded by death,
staring as some half-brained mummer
pinned a gaudy star on my hollow chest
and urged me to rise and rejoin the slaughter.

Once again I feel a bond halfway around the earth
while I hunch over a desk in my warm garret
under a snow-covered roof. He sprawls
in desert sand smelling diesel and rocket fuel,

ordnance rattling in cacophonous air,
squinting across no-man's land,
tasting blood lust risen in his throat,
the hatred he would die to unleash on his brother
whose father also sits at a desk—
an Arabic scribbler proud he never killed,
ashamed he cannot save any of those dearest ones
because they have elevated their love and hate
of him to God's will.

        Oh, Absalom, my son.

FATHERS

I see the lattice of my father's face
   in the mirror—lines from the bridge of his nose
   run under my cheeks; my forehead
   creases above his watery eyes and droopy lids.
 I scratch, laugh, and trace my
scaffolding with his gestures.
I can't hide his carpentry in my features.

You say your father played the same music,
printed with my hand, built life out
of hard work and the poetry of Roosevelt Road.
I wish I could be him—loved by the song
in your eyes when you speak of his quick turns,
read right even when I do wrong.

I tried so hard not to grow the way
my father was built. He would have demeaned
yours, rejected the music, laughed at
the printing, and ignored whatever it said.
I wanted to write him off for adoption,
just the way he took me in.

Like your father I loved the blues, booze
and ladies, yet felt my father's hatred
grown large and bitter like some choking
weed breaking down the trellis of love
we're born with in our hearts—my love
crumbled, my face a penance, myself a father.

THE BOOK CLIFFS

Rank on distant rank
  all the way to the blue mesa,
   the red and brown mountains,
  flat-topped desert cliffs,
 stand above the dusty floor,
hushed wind blowing blurred images
past the man descending the maelstrom:
the yellow-enameled cloth
of a library rebound with POUND
in shiny black blocks
from cliff tops to sandy ground.

Thomas Wolfe ran madly
in the stacks, pulling, reading,
reshelving and reading on.
James Dickey bought $300
in the Vanderbilt bookstore
and his wife testified
he'd read every one.
I try to read Joyce
in the dim light
and my eyes hurt
twice as much.

A tall Scotsman
fallen out of Boswell's "Life"
sits here comfortably,
his close-set eyes knitting
criticism out of skeins of Shakespeare,
but absolute variety
and traditional wind
push me on.

In the calm gray before dawn returns
to color the cliffs,
I sit and poke the sand,
mocked by Wolfe
singing drunkenly home:
"I wrote ten thousand words today.
I wrote ten thousand words."

BOOKSHELVES

Some people start writing by building bookshelves,
  or ease their aches for stardom by clearing
    space for an Oscar above the fireplace.
  But once begun what carries them day-to-day—
    the shelf?
the vacant space between the bookend and the picture frame?

I've written for years for no earthly end.
Oh, at first I vaguely hoped for fame,
women (well, sex) and high esteem,
but I always got more from being on the wire
alone, making it through every day on play.

It must be the effrontery that annoys me.
Before a word is set down, a gesture made,
they know there will be awards, wealth, status.
How do they, those bastards;
how can they know?

GROWL

I have seen the best minds of my generation rise to the bait
    of corporate greed as hungrily as largemouth bass breaking
      the warm waters of a Wisconsin lake to take a factory-tied fly.
Those who once thought they could make a difference pop up
    like crocuses in the steamy little condo front yards
   watered by the spray from washing Saabs and BMWs,
Those who support oil company wars so profits
   will continue to flow like crude upon the waters,
Those who snort a little coke in memory of the old days,
   play some Beatles and sing along,
   fake a couple of spastic steps that pass for white folks dancing.
Like all bourgeoisie risen from the working class,
   they resent looking into that mirror.
They blame labor for the recession and complain
   because they can't make money fast enough to get
   that second Volvo, a partnership,
   a better table at the annual country club dance.

I have seen them ambling though the corridors of power
   with all the ease of orderlies wheeling cadavers to the morgue.
I have walked through their blank stares at sunset and surf
   valued only for the height of the hotels behind them.
I have seen all the physical dexterity developed on the ball fields
   of their youth reduced to chasing useless dogs
   around public parks and trying to figure
   the best way to collect the turds in the plastic bags.
I have watched them increase the size of their TV screens
   to make the vapid images larger inside their empty heads.

They believe that Ted Koppel is wiser than Socrates.
They believe jazz is the 50-minute solo of a brain-damaged child
    tamed by the Librium of Wynton Marsalis,
that if it weren't for drugs and carnival
    we could nuke all of Central and South America,
that Asian people have found their true calling in making American
    underwear.
In their blank eyes I see fear of flat land,
    who cannot operate outside the stone skins of cities,
    who think nobody in Wyoming ever read a book,
    who believe Dakota and Oklahoma are too good for Indians,
    although they haven't been there or seen one,
    who see the face of Nature in the cross-eyed
    stares of pigeons on transit tracks.

And their chubby young sage Rush Limbaugh will not tell them
    that the money will wither in their hands,
    the oil will stick to their skins,
    the soot will collect in their lungs,
    and they will be penned inside their own bodies,
    poisoned by their own wastes they can no longer flush.

That in a century when we have defeated and resurrected
    the four horsemen of the old Apocalypse,
    we have also created the ultimate mummers parade,
    the convulsed dancers of chemical death
    filling the streets eight abreast,
    led by the four fathers of their greatest fears:
        Finance, Foolishness, Anonymity and Fat.

FINAL JUDGMENT

I worried more about death when I
   was closer to birth. Now justice eternal
      fades like some vague teenage mythology.
  I don't see any asparas in my
 post-death future; my life's not so infernal
   that I'll come back as a tyrant, rat, or snake.
All I have left of that original lie
is a sack of random maybes and venial
   sins that I no longer calculate like some
kid totaling one short of hell when I die.
Our final judgments don't appear in our journals.
   Instead of making that last note, we get
killed crossing Boylston with one eye
in the wrong direction, some ungovernable
   factory or personal hate making us blind.

While we ride past homeless kids in yards of dirt
blocks away from dumpsters full of edible
  discards outside rich people's restaurants,
children with hate-filled eyes work hands that ache
for equalizers—dope, guns, money, the thrill
   of power even if it's over just one
wretched other. Don't fault the Raider's shirt,
the rapper's cliché. The shame is capital.
   You can hide behind stone government walls
and oak desks in indifferent classrooms, shirts
with silver badges, or any livable
   places cash, hate or racism can buy.
It's not for me to tell why dessert
is served to you in your bought heaven, all
   at the expense of someone else's hell.

IN THE GOOD OLD SUMMER

Summer ran from a broad gold band
    up my yard where lush sweetness
        gathered in a tuck fold of honeysuckle
    then topped a hill and tumbled to slippery
    clay banks of creek cutting a broad
  pasture. Mud sucked at my ankles
and frogs plunked in unharmonious jumps.
Cows watched, chewed, and turned lazily away,
like adults who didn't care what we did
as long as it was in the open.

For a hundred days the sun put us
to sleep in soft grass. Sundays we sat
on the flat back of my dad's boat on
the undulating Susquehanna, bellies full
of fried chicken and iced tea, the deep river
and our middle class lives so certain
a safety net that we rolled overboard
anytime and swam in soundless oblivion.

When bright siren-streaked fire engine
parades swept through town, high school
bands from somewhere near Philly
marched up Locust street in tempos
so complex we kids ran all the way
with them just to feel that beat
do things to more than one part of us
at a time. Brighter than fire engines,
their flash and strut were the sequined
costumes we would wear if we had the rhythm
to march our town out of the 19th century.

Now I know the terrible war that can be fought
when stolid German-Americans see their
lockstep leaders mocked by Africa.
They'd turn their children into sausage
for learning to love the night, cities,
women with eyes like deep rivers and skin
richer than clay creek banks. And music.

Summertime and the living was easy,
but then we didn't know the blues,
the hawk, the hood, the line.
Some of my buddies stayed home
and never learned. Some found out
under great fiery blossoms of destruction
dug in rice paddy walls. And some of us
followed the rhythm right out
of our metronome town as easily as
we rolled into the cool dark river
and let its gentle irregular sweep
deep as some dusky soul carry us
someplace else to be born again
in the sound of the backbeat
always in the heart.

AFROBLUE

On a summer night when the world is layered
  in blue-black strata and the session in my head
   has cooled from riffling bop to a plaintive
  light blue misty tenor in a thin layer above the river,
   the sinuous melodic line slides in and out of the darkness
  weaving a string of quarter notes through the black screen
that fences you in. I stand next to the river's heavy silence
and the air is a wet curtain stirred only by song.

Jazz is musical sex, the saxophone its male instrument,
and I blow that song into you lying there,
luminescent from starlight,
languid and drowsy as an August river turning slowly,
one half tone lighter than the night,
Afroblue and chocolate brown.
Runs of sixteenths over subdued bass /Afroblue/
wind through the screen to stir you in counterpoint,
excite your strings and sound your drum /Afroblue/
a cool mint whisper in heavy chocolate,
Afroblue and you.

Stretch those strings and vibrate.
Let the sax lift you on my blue tone—rise—
starlight running like water over your sleek head
raised in the night air—flutter—
and rise a bit more—flutter—
rise up to engulf music, color, darkness,
   river, soil, blood, cry, tenor—rise and flutter—
lift your wings above the world and rise,
carry the keening of a minor chord struck
on your vibrant strings again and again and again.

Stretch the player.
Lift his eyes to the stars.
Coax him out of those abject depths that cause music
to wail against being, loneliness, the desert of night;
tease him in spite of himself to strain to a height
where it might—where he might—
rise and grasp your chest below those wings and cling.
Arch those great dark wings
and beat down the air in tympanic profusion.

He will clutch your full breasts slung under those
powerful burgeoning wings and rise with you,
his music meld to you /Afroblue/ melt into you /Afroblue/
beyond any where any man with music could hope to rise,
beyond his music,
beyond any willfulness of his own.
Afroblue melted into the rush of those great rising African wings,
torn free of earth drag on his soul,
torn free of himself, notes, scale, time and place,
carried away /Afroblue/,
sliding along one tapering arm of the galaxy
and spinning off into space,
the song of joy at being bound beneath those great wings
returned from impossibly taut strings,
deep space drum,
and tenor madness like a radio tracer from a satellite gone wild—
Afroblue, Afroblue, Afroblue, Afroblue . . .

REFLECTION

Last night in the hotel room
  I saw myself full length and naked
  in the mirror, a dumb animal
  caught by its own reflection
 on a hard surface, half admiring
 the stocky old man's decent
proportion of life and death,
muscle and sag.

I didn't want to reproduce that image,
have children like myself, catch that
reflection in the eyes of others, or
show myself how I have changed,
how much I remain the same.

I would rather be an earthen cup to give
your liquid substance form.   If
we broke the mirrors, opened our veins
to dull the water's surface, blackened the moon,
we could go about our lives unencumbered by ourselves.
If you will be dark water on the rock,
I will be stone for you to know.

THE POTTER'S MISTRESS

It's the clay that forms the potter's hand,
    patching cracks, building grooves across the fingers first,
    turning on the wheel hands into hands till
    one night he hears the hollow clink
    of his arm against the workroom sink.
That's the way the potter's owned
    (we see the cleft on sculpted stone and miss
    the bluntness left on hammering fists):
    clay malingers underneath the fleshy maul,
    forming slowly in return, the illusion
    of success in form drawn out of earth,
    hardening the potter most of all.
It's the same for red-eyed astronomers,
    machinery men who make our cars;
    thrown on the wheel, cultures inferred from shards,
    the artifacts say these men have been made our way;
    they are the amphorae raised when one no longer
    knows the music of the Plain of Jars.
That's the net effect of setting matter in motion:
    the scraped hollow up to the old man's skinny neck,
    the rasping echo of his damp insides,
    the glaze on ochre skin, fit finally
    for decorative effect and stiffened play
    (brown breasts those bowls under the
    peasant blouse of the potter's mistress there,
    and beneath her skirt. . .well-urned, you'd say?):
The potter only thinks he molds the clay.

ROSETTE

In the middle of all this mess
  I find the rosette,
    that little fragrant petaled flower
  where all tenderness is centered,
wind myself into a small cochineal
figure fitted to the concentrated flare,
spiral into the warm soft
dark heart of the miniscule rose,
rest there and sense the minute pulsing,
the anemone flow,
the delicate oxygenated exhalation
rousing me to life while I rest—
rose,
La Vie en Rose,
tiny rose,
rosette.

My delicate darling too precious to touch,
too perfect to be anything but felt,
inhaling your bright fragrance
till my senses melt together
and I touch the tip of my tongue
to the pure pearl of dew
shimmering there
in the tiniest niche,
the innermost place,
the heart of the rose,
the essence of rose,
la vie en rose,
tiny rose,
rosette.

WALTZERS

I'm the bulky acrobat upside down
   in white leotards, leather belt and wrist
     straps, knees hooked over a swaying
   trapeze, a journeyman aerialist who
   climbs every night to arc in even rhythm
and do the sure-handed catch, free release,
and clean toss for others to perform around.

You're the slotted dancer on a music
box, quickly hesitant on slim legs, skirt
swirled below dark bodice, carrying through
sharp turns on one toe, one arm arched above
your pinned hair, the other hand behind your
back. Then you move again through the set
positions of the same spastic performance.

Wound up and bound to sound,
you dance for me to drop at your feet.
Swinging slowly, heels above my head,
I wait for you to fall into my hands.

JODY AND THE TIGERS

The animals got loose while Jody
    and I were playing.
     Three tigers loll in the pasture;
    another sleeps in the arc of a fallen tree.
   The lemur hides in the bushes with eyes like
bike reflectors.
                When I capture
him, he scrambles and pushes, then crouches
in the pouch my windbreaker
makes, snuggling against
my chest.
            In the field, her hair aswirl,
Jody pushes an orang-
ou-tang between the shoulder blades,
saying in her croaky voice, "Go home, Ting."
He lingers, eyes three-quarters low,
knuckles dragging in the meadow.

The sleeping tiger's ear is soft and prickly
in my fist.
            I pull him up;
the other three fall into step,
ignoring the quiet stares
of the bears who find their own
way home.
            I am five with a fifty-
year-old heart aching because
it should always be this way: tired
after play, waking the tigers
and walking them home.

DEATH IN VENICE, CALIFORNIA

The old man sits on a metal folding chair at the beach
   in the pale winter sun. His eyes scan the volleyball
   game blurred by the babes on rollerblades,
his hands lying limp on a lump in his lap.

 And he dreams of a teenager drifting
in a wooden rowboat on the sluggish Susquehanna,
a fishing rod braced on the gunwale,
the butt end chocked under his instep,
sitting opposite a firm-breasted high school girl
so fresh and new she didn't know
the first long pubic hair crept out of the cuffed leg
of her canvas shorts or that the lump in his pants
was as hard as the oar in his hands.

Now all his dividends are paid on investments
made long ago. His rate of interest is the same,
but he is satisfied with reverie of the time
when he could drop the oar, toss the rod
in the boat and jump across to that hot-bodied
woman who stared at him with eyes that burned
like a match held too long.

He found out where that hair led,
and even if he can't reach out quick
and grab the lithe ladies on the rollerblades,
he knows he once had as much of someone as he wanted,
and studied her for as long as he cared to
in brilliant summer sun.

CISTERNS

An old man sleeps on a cafe table,
  his arms sprawled in front of him.
   Inside his head two tiny girls
  dance on the table top, dark woodsy
 maidens in diaphanous forest green
with little lamps inside their eyes.

From a nearby table a gentle brown lady
smiles at the old man as though she
can see the tiny dancing girls and loves
that part of the man who cannot do anything
except let those wood nymphs whirl.

Bus stop people outside mostly ignore
the old man except for a couple
with not-yet-frozen smiles who look
to see if he is breathing and would not
disturb his warm place dream
or force him to walk out in winter.

The brown lady across tries a few notes
on the chilly air, laughs at herself
in a section of mirror, and matches her piece
of reflection with a larger fragment of song.
A bus carries off the kind couple and several
of the oblivious; the brown lady sings the song
the tiny girls in the man's head dance to.

We cannot touch the earth in these asphalt places,
but let us praise the wellsprings of those magical ones
who sit like cisterns in these dry cities
and bubble up dance, song, and tiny spirit lights
like votive candles at the altars
inside the sleepy heads of old men no one knows.

HOME

"HOME IS THE PLACE WHERE, WHEN YOU HAVE TO GO THERE,
THEY HAVE TO TAKE YOU IN."
—ROBERT FROST, *THE DEATH OF THE HIRED MAN*

Some of the best hours of my youth were spent in bars.
Away from my so-called peers
I learned to grasp the essence of slurred speech,
plumb the depths of a lost soul,
look tall people in the eye.
By the age of twelve I had an advanced degree
in enduring the special interests
of people who weren't interesting to me.
I could slip out of a heavy-handed embrace
as easily as the high-flyer tumbles to the next trapeze.
And I loved it.

Today the smell of stale beer,
the sting of cigaret smoke,
the too-sweet undertone of too much cologne turn me on.
I feel larger, livelier, sharper.
I love jazz I can barely understand,
people who lounge on swivel stools
and speak with throaty voices, knowing eyes,
and endless streams of talk.
I don't always understand them.
I don't always understand me.
But there's nowhere else I can find that home feeling
when I can't stay at home.

And only a select few are left.
The booze business is dying.
VCRs entertain those badly educated in the schools.
But when everyone lives alone in a condo,
when we're down to the final saloon
on the most obscure street
in the hardest-to-get-to part of the city,
you will find me leaning there,
foot cocked on the rail,
bourbon glass in hand,
charter member of the last family in town.

ANGELS

FOR RON FOREMAN

"STILL THROUGH CLOVEN'D SKIES THEY COME,
THEIR PEACEFUL WINGS UNFURLED."
—HARK, THE HERALD ANGELS SING

Two drinkers talk about angels
 they have known in Christmases past.
Their backs to the drafty door they sit,
forearms on the bar, sweaters flared at their hips,
heads inclined, remembering not
skinny blond angels with blue eyes,
but those with full-lipped cherubic faces
in great clouds of dark hair with smoldering eyes.

Somewhere between the angels' wings that beat
terror through alcohol-soaked brains
and those transparent-eyed breastless blonds
holding brass trumpets on cathedral walls,
these men have known real angels of love
and mercy, tenderness and passion—
ephemeral beings now for all their soothing wings.

Late on winter nights when holiday glitz
and fat-mouthed cheer can drive despair
deep into the heart, they are given hope
against debasement and the greater
portion of their experience by fiercely-held
memories of distant angels who had breasts,
thighs, hot fathomless eyes for them,
and visited grace upon the bitter corners
of the world where these men must do their best.

FRAYED PLAID ROBES

While my father strutted ghostlike
  on the broad ramparts of his life,
    his greatest truths lurked in dark corners.
    The more he thought he knew what was around,
  the more realities scurried along the edges,
quick furtive things he could only guess at.

In his last days my father saw farmers move
in weird dances where only cornshocks stood.
He dodged imaginary slaps
and cars that never came down the street.
He talked to people across the room
as if they came from different worlds.

I walk into the VA hospital every Monday
and stare my future in the face.
Ashy old men shuffle past in frayed plaid robes,
cigarets burning down to yellowed knuckles.
They mumble meaningless conversations
with absent passersby in vacant hallways.
Someday I'm going to be a shambling phantom
in an unfurnished future.

I fear the loss of fire, but the nurses tell me
that, drugged and alcoholed, these men
never felt the rage to dare life's tightropes.
Still, I get an attitude about the broad
daylight truths that scare us into doing right
while the tough rat-like facts of life
gnaw at the foundations, pick at
the threads on the frayed plaid robes
until we stand naked and alone
in front of our graves wondering,
How did we come to this?

DISORGANIZATION

My doctor tells me the new hitch in my heartbeat is inexplicable,
   but it disturbs my sleep
    and is connected to that slight cough when I am tired.
   Not to be confused with the old hitch in my heartbeat
  from most of the seventies spent on speed,
 or that other slight cough
from thirty years of pipe smoking and fat cigars.

My father echoed his father:
it's not the growing old that bothers me
but the falling apart that goes with it.
They both broke down like old factories,
their machinery chocked and shimmed
to tolerances no caulking could pad,
their dynamos gone eccentric,
powering down,
their foundations shattered by vibrations.
Dust and gunk clogged the sump pumps and generators
until their tattered roofs collapsed,
their doors flapped in least wind,
and they were defenseless against the rain.

This is not a sympathy plea.
You will understand that when it happens to you.
I only come out on days when I feel all right.
I stay home when my blood feels like oatmeal,
my lungs like wet sponges,
my head like the clouds east of some industrial town,
my prick a withered stopcock
dripping hot acid down a tin leg.

On days like that it's enough to make a man
scrape together transit fare to step in front of the train.
But the tough old guys go for the good days as long as they can,
even though they see the world through weepy eyes,
resent their limbs for their fundamental unyielding awkwardness,
hate their teeth because they will outlast them.

There's no shame in growing old,
but don't you young people try to tell us how hard life is.
We may hear a certain world-weariness in your voices,
but we feel it deep in our bones.

AT THE DENTIST

At first it's like standing below Mt. Rushmore,
  huge immobile faces above,
    until the pinch and penetration
  of Novocaine flips the relationship.
  Then I become stone-faced,
 and like Borglum and his crew,
they put on gloves and goggles
and set to work with picks and drills.

Metal edges scream against rock solids,
cooling spray haloes the air;
I am Teddy Roosevelt with a *rigor mortis* smile,
cutters just below my eyelid,
eccentric whir carving my teeth.

I sit in an immobilizing chair.
Lights and armatures angle away yet
wait at hand: technology circumventing honesty.
I don't need the inevitable Daumier on the wall,
the dazzling happy tooth brushing its moronic top,
re-runs of *Marathon Man*.

We had two dentists in my home town.
Doc Myers laid on the tongs,
stood on my chest and pulled.
When I survived, I got a shot of whisky.
Doc Brockley never hurt anybody.
He's the reason I'm here every day this week.
Hard things need hard ways.

While the drill screams through the bones of my skull,
fine spray wets my face,
and bits of tooth arc away from the excavation,

I try to find my favorite drill.
The high whine of the fine grade
shrinks me when friction turns to burning.
The coarse irregular one suits my style,
but I think it gouges out too much.
The tongue exaggerates everything.

I fade out to the mosquito buzz inside my ear,
one-sided conversations, bubbling water,
the rattle of stainless steel on glass,
until a drop forge forces an inlay
into a cauterized root canal.

"Rinse," says the dental tech,
and blood and calculus swirl down the drain
like the end of a shower at the Bates Motel.
We who narrowly escape
stare in shock at the high cost of crude
work to fix a failed body part,
and go to lunch to chew on our tongues.
While back in dark torture chambers,
rich dentists contemplate suicide.

ON THE BUTTON

"...IT IS TOWARD THE DISINTEGRATION OF HUMAN GROUPS
THAT BATTLE IS DIRECTED."
                    —JOHN KEEGAN, *SIX ARMIES IN NORMANDY*

smooth round plastic
  black, white, gray
 green on my touchtone

consider the evolution of the button
its golden age the shirt stud
high buttons on shoes and corsets

buttons galore in its great middle age
with eyes of their own lashed
to hold them in their holes

an age of plenty when buttons
were adornments, symmetrical trim
abundant on a sailor's pants

a brief uselessness before
(button up, button down, push)
the corporate button

spawn of history and electricity
faceless buttons, numbered buttons
in rows ranks lines and sets

the panic button
THE button
button, button, who's got...

the ON button opens false worlds:
TV, TRON, data
they push our buttons

room temperature facts
buttons systematically destroy
place, time, taste, smell

telephone calls:
the only button-
related reality

OFF is the only answer
move a little closer
we can unbutton civilization

scatter bits of memory:
sow fear, chaos, confusion in the logic
forbid them touch the Apple

ODYSSEUS

Weariness with life makes young men attractive;
  old men require youthful vigor: such is expected
    when a warrior comes home. Under a green tree,
  before I walk the lane to claim the place above
the river, I rest my sword and wooden shield.
 These new trees repeat murmurs of hope and sweeten
shade for short rests. Live or fallen, old trees
teach hard ways: bend only with the grain. Water
runs past the house where they let voices like
the breeze blow through in mindless variation.
My name has a life of its own; in my namelessness,
back from trying to return, I will be restored
a wife and take up household ways: choose food,
games and times and spin stories from the raw wool
of my adventures, daily tussle with a woman
schooled in how much she can get away with, who
will cede the exquisite pain of sweet submission
when she has gone too far. It is not because
I lack understanding of domestic life that I have
stayed so long unhoused. Soon I will be too old
to see the children grown. I can play with the
dark-eyed moppet on the Persian rug, twist her
straight black hair, gauge the sunlight on golden
skin, but will I teach her how to draw a bow,
catch fish by watching, defeat enemies by direct
action instead of guile? If I cannot begin the life
I would have in less warlike times, I can go on.
I say I am too old, but this way agrees with me;
I can follow it till death, but that yet unsuccessful
way I must first try—to call for entry at my own
door, understand a wife, be patient with children,
break nothing, not look back nor far ahead.

Freedom cannot be an eternal *no* to some relentless
domestic *yes*. I do not fear sailing through a homey
storm as much as letting the calm lull me into
unwatchfulness. Water never takes us home. The wind,
a mistress with greater variety than man can master,
is quick to lie, charm, or force us to new tricks
in ancient places. Leaving those lonely ones along
the way, each a hurt in an old heart not so hungry
yet unsatisfied, I am touched by the sting of old
scars, aches in my bones. Still, I have done wonderful
things: from the top of an eastern temple seen a great
muddy river turn to gold, crouched beside wild dogs
and tasted the northern sea, squatted among early merchants
and scooped soft white rice and sticky vegetables off
banana leaves, caught goats on stony cliffs, had tropic
maidens weave hibiscus in my hair. But as I tell the children,
I have not yet heard the sun hiss when it hits the western
sea. Many times were bad, but like any discoverer who climbs
a hill and wrongly names a distant ocean, I call this life
my own. A man who chooses cannot complain. I will take up
my weapons and carry them home. If there is not a child
to sing to, no wife to hold me while I doze, no excitement
in a safe bed, no purpose to my dreams, I know the words
of the wind, the paths across water, how to sail away.
Now, an old gardener deaf to airy promises, I plant trees.

MYTHOLOGY

Among others, Freud and the Greeks agree
   we must kill our fathers and love our mothers.
    But I think Greek mythology was an elaborate parlor game
   played by the idle rich to suit their own lives.
  I see Athena on water skis,
 playing basketball for the normal school,
getting kicked in the ass by Zeus
because she wouldn't bring the cows home.
She marries Hephaestus, the misshapen craftsman—
I know that's not the traditional scenario.
It's Aphrodite who weds the artificer,
producing Eros, but the cosmic board game
was probably played a million times,
and we've handed down only one version,
when we should be creating our own. Every life
is a different set of circumstances,
and the only way to win
is to match your luck to your hand.

So I killed the man who made things,
traveled my odyssey while he died,
and came home to hear my mother say,
"You don't have to sleep on the floor anymore."
That's one circle I'd leave Thebes to miss closing,
one more prophecy spurned for fear,
and travel spurred by hope that Fate is the road,
our final resting only where we are after
some accident has stopped us, and the auguries
of our parents turn out to be our lives
cast in flesh by their craft and love,
teaching us to fly and knowing where we'll fall.

THE BITCH GODDESS

She came on the train at 79th Street,
  low round leather cap stuck on short hair,
    her head a block of volcanic rock holding obsidian eyes.
  Tight leather jacket zipped high,
 she wore studded wrist bands, stone jeans,
 and black boots with shiny pointed tips.
If God is a woman, this was her Satanic counterpart,
the devil goddess of the material world
decked out in rough clothes and a homicidal attitude.
She was every man's nightmare, the subway Medusa.
Look at her wrong and she'd chop you down,
kick you out the door, and spit on the spot on the floor.

That is, if she'd let go
of the three-year-old with the huge silent eyes.
The fist of the meanest woman on the South Side
held delicately a tiny hand stuck out of a rich purple coat.
On brand new blue leather shoes, the little girl walked
as though one misstep could cause earthquakes.
The woman faced the inside of the el car
and held the chrome pole as if she
were now in charge of the train.
The other hand gently supported
the child swaying in the aisle.
In a minute the child turned,
her mother pulled her up to the seat,
and big eyes focused on shiny blue shoes.

I leaned forward to the little girl and said,
"Those are some pretty shoes you have."
She smiled, then her head snapped up
to the goddess of destruction from the black South
who already had me set in the gunsights of her eyes,
her free hand working at some imaginary murdering instrument.

I have seen the sides of mountains blown off
and muddy fronts of California hills break away
and obliterate houses and highways. When a glacier
calves, the high weathered front crumbles,
and a new face, clean, cool and pure appears.
Something like that happened across the aisle.
The stone face of the bitch goddess
collapsed into a rosy smile.
She said softly, "It's her first el ride."
The little girl smiled and shook her head emphatically.
All the way to the Loop the mother and I
talked like old friends, while the child
discovered a larger world with lots of colors.

THE BEATS

The Beats spent a lot of energy defining Beat
  with their V-8 cross-country
    charging-at-space between any place
  and walked or half ran or took little steps
  and looked four ways at one time to see
the next word on a light pole, store front,
snatch of jazz or pieces of air.

They moved it on their tongues
like some leprosy-white Henry Miller holy
communion and tilted it to street lights
as another bright fragment of a definition
not yet made whole, just like
the ragged openings of a baggy-pants old
queen poet's body can be perfect
God-like segments of meaning—
meaning, the meaning , the Mean
Ning, powerman of the cartoon
Shazaam and Marie McDonald whose
perfect blond goddess body
was another part of the meaning,
the Mean Ning. . .till the fragments
built up a sequence of Mean Ning,
and meaning faded and what was left
was the beat
  Beat,
    on the beat,
after the beat, beat on the road,
beat on the beat, beatbeat,
the beat, beat anybeat, but
hard beat, and meat beat, back beat,
beatbeat, get beat, catch the beat,
stomp on the beat, beatbeat,

beat on the street, deep beat,
down beat, beat down,
beaten down, down beat, man,
like get down, man, like beaten down, man,
like get down is only
a beat to start,
jump beat, beat start,
start beat, beatbeat, heartbeat, get beat
on the road beat, do beat, love beat
drunk beat, drum beat, beatbeat.

Beat is what you are after the downbeat.
You can't get beat below the roadbeat.
Beat into the asphalt
you become the beat in somebody else's tires,
a beat only other Beats can hear,
back beat, beatbeat, to be beat or be beaten
down,
as in down,
as in down, man,
but hip,
down,
beat and hip after bop,
not beat up but afterbeat bop,
too beat for cool, too beat for bop,
but hip to it all
before the hop.

TEACHING

What did I do all those years?
  Don't you remember?
  Third grade, $8 \times 4 = 32$.
  Sixth grade, "It was many and many a year ago..."
 Tenth grade, *Julius Caesar, The Mill on the Goddamned Floss*
College?
Who introduced you to Anaïs Nin, Lou Salome, Sappho,
Senghor, George Herbert, Cortázar?
You don't remember?
$8 \times 12 = 96$, Mr. Brown.
"Had I not loved Rome more?" That was me.
The Steps of the Pentagon.
Doctor Brown, Professor Brown, Old Doc Brown.

Am I faded now like some cloudy corner of a chalkboard
or a grainy desk top where all you can see
are Bill Rednor's initials carved in the corner?
I remember all of you.
For me it's like standing on a low summer hill,
infinite blue dome of possibility above,
and all the wildflowers of the season dancing in the warm breeze.
  "The world stands out on either side,
   no wider than the heart is wide.
   Above the world is stretched the sky
   no higher than the soul is high." —Edna St. Vincent Millay
The first time you heard that was from me!

There, Sarah Kobs, bright-eyed daisy,
the best poet I ever taught.
Wilma Campbell, tough-stalked black-eyed susan
whose parents were the only ones to dare

cold North Philly streets for a parent-teacher conference.
Al Schulze, high school wrestler, tunnel rat,
the first one of mine on that obscene wall in Washington.

It's not the mass murderers
and big city politicians we teachers remember;
their lives were set before we met them.
It's the ordinary people, the regular ones who
wanted to get something for themselves,
make a little difference,
these are the ones.

If you want to write western novels,
I know just the guy in Montana to talk to.
Want to re-build the Oakland Expressway?
I know just the woman in Dallas to call.
Sure, they didn't learn all that from me,
but they learned,
and I helped a little.

When the sun hits its highest angle,
I see the ones I did touch moving proudly
across a grand expanse of land—
primary colors, prime numbers,
premier poets, so proud
so proud,
even I can almost feel it.

MADNESS, A MEDIATION ON A STUDENT'S EXCUSE

After a two-week absence
   this student comes into my office,
   sits in the chair opposite me,
and tells me that he is a paranoid schizophrenic
and spring is difficult for him.

What kind of excuse is that?
I'm manic-depressive
and it's hard for me all year round.
On sunny days there's too much wind;
snow is beautiful but cold and hard to drive in.
Every friend I've got has screwed up sooner or later.
Ever lover I ever married turned out to be a wife.

And don't blame it on the medication;
you're obviously not on mine, and I won't do yours.
Thorazine turns me into a zombie.
Lithium screws up my natural rhythm.
Librium turns me into a bombardier—
look at all the pretty explosions way down there!
Booze doesn't help:
every time I get drunk I remember everything
that happened the last time I got drunk.

So straighten up, young man.
You can try being some psychotic Billy the Kid
and terrorizing everyone around here,
but I'm Sheriff Pat Garret, and this is my territory.
When I'm manic, I'll enjoy putting the screws to you;
when I'm depressive, I'll do a thorough job.
So you'd better get to work
because nobody rides out of here uneducated.

YOU, JOHN KEATS

This weak-chested wheeze
that powers the fever
up my face and into my head
like a drywood boiler generating steam
propelling me through
monthlong thickets of experience
whirring by in cacophonies
of autumn colors strewn on plush turf
brilliant sun fits crowning my hot head
like a torturer's hat,
blinded without, blinding within,
shattering my vision so each step
bumps the kaleidoscope
at the dark tunnel's end of my sight.

The taste of leaves is smoke.
The smell of smoke dilates my nostrils.
The warm air flumes,
mixes drywood and dead leaves,
dirt and onion grass,
broad heavy base of pine,
leathery tree bark,
fish on sea air
into a great autumnal chowder boiling inside my head
above the hearth fire in my chest,
my squat legs sturdy on the stone floor,
my stumpy arms hooked for hanging things,
my crazed consciousness a woodsman's cookbook,
my sad congested heart
singing like a stone at the center of the cauldron.

For all the majestic chords of Nature's symphony
scrambled by perceptual madness,
broadcast in my raving awareness,
for all that I might care to be or cured,
I gather myself in quiet writing
while my senses are dragged behind fall's runaway cart
and I wish, oh wish, oh declare,
if I were half my age
and twice as mad
as all the music played at once,
I would be you, John Keats;
I would be you.

AMULET

Like a rock star's amulet,
    polished and vague on a silver chain,
    such is the moon I have for you.

  What designs, symbolic scenes of hunt or love
 that may have been on it, are long since
worn to soft bulges and indentations.

A rat has chewed the rim.

How can I give you this insignificant,
this worn and tattered disk
grown inferior by is own use,
by its own hand,
if this clockface once had hands.

I sit in the Golden Nugget Pancake House
at Broadway and Racine
on the 12th day of the 11th month
while Armistice signers board their trains,
old soldiers are deloused,
truculent fascists walk sullenly away,
and cummings has come home again,
seeds of Baudelaire in his fecund heart.

It's like the day after a funeral:
cards to answer, flowers for the church,
bills to pay, clothes to give away,
relatives to send back home.

Joe, a former flyweight contender,
paces between the window and the counter's end,
muttering to himself in a foreign tongue.
The man next to me smells of mothballs.
The pretty young woman in fur dances nervously at the phone,
trying to find out when her lover's train will arrive,
if her lover's train will come,
and calculates the distance to the ladies' room.

My moon, strong as any Wordsworth knew,
shines through these blasted trees,
climbs the wall,
throws light enough for winter nights.

I cannot afford a silver chain,
but I will give you this moon,
soft as a silver dollar pancake.

Slid in your direction, this ragged, bitten,
mothballed thing rings on the countertop.
You could wear it on a string.

SPEED BUMPS

TO J. KOVAR

I don't hold with those who hear birthdays
   as rumble strips on the highway of age.
  Look out the speed bumps say, toll ahead.
 For most of us it's been pay as you go all along.
 The only perspective that comes with age
is that of all passersby—scenic views,
pieces of history, silly roadside attractions
vaguely seen and faintly remembered.
Old folks sit in McDonald's at 10 a.m.
and talk to each other for the comfort
of knowing they saw the same things.
All clichés are true. We become our parents
to whom we are always children. We become
Lear, and if we're lucky, the Fool, too.
He's the one who tells us there's a hitch
in the heart beat before we admit it.
He sees death in young faces and loves them.
Beyond excuses, he knows our lovers
lie because they love us. It's only a fair game
if we uncover a deceit of our own
for every friend we have known.

Blossoms fall outside my window
and I think of those already gone.
Live fast, love hard, don't die young,
and this is what you become.
All my regrets are for excess.
I'm still the traveler halfway to St. Louis
before I ask why we're going.

I look across the wild moor and see
the bent backs of my betters,
hear wracked coughs and tired mumblings.
I act out their ragged movements to try on aging.
Late one night I sat with a bartender sage,
playing Lear to his Fool, and it all came down to this:
most roads are never taken
and we choose the only ones we can.
We see the present through the mists of time.
For the sweep of history our own thumbnail
biographies read convenient fictions after the fact.
It was all set from the day we popped
into the world and wailed to go back.

This may be said for the accumulation of age:
it gives the appearance of wisdom grown out
of experience and masks from the young
the truth that we never had much skill.
Our formative years occur when our parents
are at the heights of their powers.
That our growth parallels their decline
is a lesson we never fully learn.
It's by the fires within us
that we most often get burned.

Even though I see rumble strips on the highway,
they always sound too loud. In parking lots
I cross speed bumps too fast. The road ahead
is better illuminated by the burning bridge behind,
but some things are always surprises. Macbeth,
brought to bay, put on his gear and yelled, "Blow, wind!
Come wrack! At least we'll die with harness on our back."

Like dead end kids the old men go.
Some mope and whine their days away.
Some of us keep on driving,
Lears for any Fool who comes our way.
No matter if our daughters are dead because of us,
if our heritage has been squandered
before our sons can make it pay,
if our dearest melodies cannot be sung
in cracked voices, if our wastefulness has turned
the very road on which we go into speed bumps
which slow us every step we take.

When the moor has sunken into weed-choked ravines,
the Fool's voice become indistinguishable from the wind,
all those we loved so far gone that we doubt they were
anything but tricks of memory, we do only what we have
practiced every day—put out a foot and find the way.
If we stand still, if we plan to rest all night and listen
to even the wisest Fool's talk, before moonrise
we suffer the ghost's demise,
loss of voice and ear, the death of poetry.
If we don't see the warning, we will miss the surprise.

BUDDY BOLDEN

A blood red sun rising makes
  a black river run blue.
    Stevedores and draymen drag themselves alive
  while the last jazz notes of the night
lie down in the dawn and die.

From the cemetery across the river
the people could hear him, they say.
I know the music, but I wish
I could have heard Buddy Bolden play.

Inside bright back doors of morning kitchens
old ladies cook up ambrosia
from white families' table scraps.
They grumble, spit and hum sweet tunes
and never touch their head wraps,
and every note of their lives, they say,
was something Buddy Bolden could play.

At the barber shop folks sang,
"I thought I heard Buddy Bolden say,
'Get out of here, take it away.'"
But they'd have let him cut their ears off
just to hear Buddy Bolden play.

On the 4th of July, 1900,
the most fertile seed unplanned
started a plant that grew up the Mississippi
and flowered across the land.
The raucous voice of Louis Armstrong
blended with the finesse of Sidney Bechet.
Ten thousand masters have been recorded now,
but you can't hear Buddy Bolden play.

POE WAS WRONG

FOR SERGIO

I always think of her head laid open
   like a cabbage—white skin and blond hair peeled
   back, brain exposed and indistinct, her wasted
 body in a fetal curl, eyes milky,
mouth hung open on one side and drooling,
her hand a claw. A lovely young woman
turned into a stuffed hawk—talons clasped,
eyes gone to glass, legs frozen, wings of the
afterlife burgeoning out of her curved back.

The red carnations became a bad joke,
like out-of-place floral trim at the edge
of an Audubon, a splash of color
on a Kolwitz, the terrified inmate
reduced to skull, skin, inchoate moans,
until by some miracle of release
she was transmuted to ash in a frozen
coffee can in the Polish cemetery.

We who love clumsily and craft our old
age in middle years sometimes settle
for dried flowers. We want them to outlast
us so we can have them near as long as
we are here. When we can't, we must love them
as much as we can before they go and not
engage in the competition for grief.

Poe was wrong. The best subject for poetry
is not the death of a beautiful woman—
not if you have to watch it happen.

THOREAU'S LAST WORDS

FOR LEE ALLEN WILLIAMS

furnace blower stops

  owl's voice
      velvet on satin sky
  even tho
storm windows are still on
  walls well insulated

short-syllabled mourning dove
              hoo-ho-hoo-hoo
  baritone quail
      ghost in gray woods

if I could sleep in trees

      moon
        burning wildness
      into my face

tramp snorting to the creek
      in mornings

      become
      "moose. . . Indians"

I would die dumber than
        the sky's chorus
  to   the
owl's requiem

JOHN BERRYMAN'S GHOST

"Many opinions and errors in the Songs are to be referred
not to the character of Henry, still less to the author,
but to the title of the work."
                                                    —77 Dream Songs

The first time, a sexy preppie from Poughkeepsie
 pressed against me at a cocktail part in Texas,
certain there dwelt beneath roughly similar
outsides similes of soul. He was alive then, so
she wasn't seeking clues to suicide. Maybe it's
apparent to those who knew him—eyes focused
by glasses, lips nested in a shaggy beard,
the right words surrounded by so much talk.

The last one said, "I'm in one of the dream songs,
I think," a wisp of immortality as long as those
cloudy constructions float on. After class
they talked for hours in crowded places. Now she
settles for our synecdoche, yet craves a leap
to the storyteller's realm where dying grandfathers,
adolescent pain, the thrill of vague uncertainty,
and golden time all turn out better in lyric tense,
if we could be here without knowing we were us.

I don't entertain as well among the coffee spoons.
My heart won't hold us above the center ring,
the sawdust mess for one afternoon. I sing my
dreams in sleep. My life no longer a death-defying
feat, there's no point in performing if they
must put up the net. I want to be on the ground
when I let go. Circuses have their own not-too-
demeaning social security for those who won't
go out alone. My talk fills the everyday hunger you
cure with your face—peanuts, crackerjacks—
while we rue the loss of arabesques in space.

RAKING LEAVES

The fourteen-year-old inside writes
  a paper on *Our Town,* and I'm out
    in a small town's big yard,
  head bent and shoulders hunched,
making the long draw across thick
fall grass, flimsy bamboo slats
gathering dry confetti in slanted sunlight.

Linden leaves like ragged parchment,
red oaks, flat golden maples,
sycamores curled like tobacco leaves—
the soft woods are bare but the beech
still holds half its load above.
I drag the rake in methodical
pulling together, heaping
the crashed assets of spring's investment.

Sweat falls in my eyes; my bifocals
blur the swirling mass; the sun
glares and magnifies the mosaic;
I get lightheaded in clear air
as my fat heart pumps, dusty
earth smells crawl up my nose,
thrashing fills my ears, insects drone,
and it's like a couple of hits of windowpane.

I don't want to get all Romantic:
a few days on the banks
of the Susquehanna is not exactly
Wordsworth in the Lake Country,
but there's some of that if I factor in
egocentricity and the city child
getting hits of small town life through homework.

When I was his age, this was also
my grandmother's yard, and I learned
how to use a bedspread
to transport tons of leaves
to the burn pile in the alley.
Today we sweep them into the gutter
and trashmen take them away.
(We've got plastic crates
for everything that isn't plastic.)

But the air still hums the way
it did before I knew what acid was;
the colors whirl about me as we do
our dervish dance through the afternoon.
Only when artificial moons glow
along the block and motley surrenders to night
do I put aside my rake, go inside,
and take up my grandmother's pen.

THE FARMHOUSE

She sits in the warm circle of the hurricane lamp,
  ruby lips, sleek black hair, the line along
   the nape of her neck and shoulder flowing into
  a flowered gown fallen around her arms.
  Perhaps she turns a lock around her finger
or tugs it through a mother-of-pearl-handled brush,
her eyes deep and dreamy, the pot pourri gown
hardly covering the rising globes of her breasts.

In such a place weather doesn't matter. I tramp
through drifts blown high at the shingled corner,
kick off rubber boots, hang my mackinaw on a peg,
and shake a halo of cold in front of the fire
before I kneel and lay my head in her lap.
Or it might be a night when fireflies ascend
from fresh grass under apple trees, thick sweet
blossom smell blowing in on the tide of spring.

Or a hot night when bugs bang screens, and after
a cool bath a fringe of perspiration lines her upper lip,
her hand is damp on the brush handle, and she
endures the lamp's heat only till I find her, and we
lie on the hooked rug by the cold stone hearth.
Damn the stubborn soil and indifferent implements!
Weather never the way crops need it, livestock diseases,
stone fences crumbling into fields! Damn the cows!

Get me that farmhouse, and I'll go till 90
with a 14-year-old heart. Ephemeral things like time
and weather, grain and soil, can't match the flat
stone foundation of a good woman and a solid house,
a round of passion deeper than the day's labor,
and love to make the seasons greedy for their days.

FOG

Men vaporize from the waist down;
    mist halos women's hats;
        horses kick and fade before they reach the woods.
    I expect stately deer in a ghostly line along the river
    startling ducks out of their own clouds,
  the hawk falling like a piece torn from low sky
to rip a gray squirrel from a snowbank.

In this watery air voices die,
horse sounds roll to a stop at the fence,
traffic is some distant rustle
like motorboats that ride the surface,
trees beyond the river,
my love asleep behind the wooden door.

At night lights diffuse to huge globes
broken into droplets at their edges,
bright pellets circling vague centers.
The owl atop the stable coos in soft rivulets into the darkness,
fluttering his barred wings to settle again
and float above the restless horses,
chomping wet hay in sea caves below.

It is winter by the sea
where men must still work away from home.
There are no land marks beyond the light,
no other ships upon this surface line between
the airy sea above, the thicker sea below.
One yields sharp-winged, beaked and noisy fish,
the other slippery silent silver tons,
where all men's skill is done by memory
and women wait where a widow's walk is but an ornament.

I shuffle waist deep through cottony sea,
my clogged head brushing through the fog,
my breath a wool scarf wound round your soft shoulders,
warm even when it is wet.

FORGET TO REMEMBER

I remember feelings so well and forget
   the events that brought them into being,
    like the thrill of the air between trapezes,
   talks with my elders about days gone by.
  My father recalled in detail being caught
in a storm and the only way to keep our
boat from being swamped was to run into
the wind. Would the gale tail off before
we were wrecked on rocks in the narrows?

All I remembered was a young woman
shivering next to me, her shoulder under my
arm, the cool skin of the bottom of her breast
resting atop my index finger, the mix of fear,
love and need for reassurance sent straight
into my chest, the way I've come to know
it in every good love in my life.

It's not what you make me remember
but what I forget when I'm with you—
basic, necessary things like eating, my name,
where the sidewalk meets the street. I
turn on the hot water faucet and stand
amazed as the liquid stream gets cold.
When I can hear, feel, and see you lying
on the other side of the wall, why must I
walk through the doorway to get
to you? When we're at work ten miles apart,
your voice is as close as my ear, your lips
on my neck, your breath inside my chest.

SECRETARY OF WAR, 1862-65

We get accustomed, as we age, to lapses
   and close-but-incorrect associations.
      We devise tricks to compensate
   for loss of facile wit and nimble memory.
   But our great middle-age strength,
the treacherous key to our mastery of quick kids,
resides in fully realized complexities.
The young leap to catch the stars,
and we hold constellations.
When they grasp galaxies,
our minds tremble at the limits of the universe.

Then one Sunday over the double acrostic
I look into the memorial distance and find,
instead of the diorama at Gettysburg,
not exactly the void—it doesn't happen that quickly—
but a growing darkness that,
because I haven't looked in some time,
seems so profound.

I can visualize the Peach Orchard from Little Round Top,
the dry grass where Pickett's men charged,
the twisted body in the Devil's Den.
I can recite the miles of track and days it took
for Hoffman's engineers to sweep the carnage
and salvage the wreckage of that victorious army.
I hang on to tight patches like the postcard
view of Fort Sumpter from the Charleston breakwater,
dour Ben Butler's post in New Orleans,
the sharp bend of the Mississippi
below the bluffs at Vicksburg.

Like some 1840s cadet at West Point studying Napoleon,
I once lay bundled in an upper bunk in a wintry lodge
with a dusty copy of Douglas Southall Freeman's
biography of Lee, applying Stonewall Jackson's
deployment of Stuart's cavalry in the Shenandoah
to chess and beating my father for the first time.

I carried a crimson and gold paperback
of Fletcher Pratt's *Ordeal by Fire* when my bicycle troops
rode red dirt hills after grade school.
I never heard a military name more inspiring than
Pierre Gustave Tousant Beauregard.
My heart still aches at the honor, loyalty,
gallantry, and invention of Robert E. Lee.
How many times I have related my plain, forward foolishness
to Grant's breaking out of a cornfield on a reconnoiter
at Shiloh and realizing that the raggedy band across from him
were Rebs, just as they saw the bluecoated general
materialize in front of them.

My eyes were always at field level.
Stone Mountain, Lookout Mountain
were too far above sticky red in army wool.
The highest I'd raise my sight was to second story holes
in downtown Gettysburg, a chance overshot,
like my hometown's burning the bridge
that turned Lee's army away from the Susquehanna
and sent them into battle from the northeast
to meet Meade's men catching up from the southwest.
So I learned that south and north,
like all political designations,
mean nothing in war.

I never felt I knew it all, or even knew one side half right,
but I once had this great divided tapestry woven in threads
of gray and silver, blue and gold, crimson, dust, steel and blood,

horse colors and bummers' rags,
great broad bands of black, tufts of cotton,
folk music with a bridle's jingle,
and hymns with martial tread.
Its watery borders held blockade runners,
ironclads, flatboats, barges, and gun boats.
Its theme: that even in fratricidal conflict
men destroyed each other for the noblest principles.
The whole thing smelled of fetid hospitals,
rancid wounds, gunpowder.
Armies of rivers against the might of states:
Potomac, Cumberland, Missouri,
Virginia, Alabama, Carolina.

I heard the brown clatter of Phil Sheridan's cavalry,
tasted wet wool on my collar at Antietam,
felt dried blood stick to my side in the Wilderness.
Just as Stephen Crane had without being there,
I saw dark riders go down the purple ravine
and merge with the black river.
Paint streaks on topographical tables dissolved
to rippling grass bent by the pointed tread of boots,
muskets rattled, death smelled sickenly sweet,
the sweat of frightened men was not like that of horses.

Now like a siren tearing through the moan of night,
pain along the seams of my skull,
the blackness of alcohol-anesthetized memory,
I have forgotten so much my life is only
ragged scraps of pain, amnesia, foolishness, and glory.

HILLSIDE

to Clem Young

Over fifty is learning how foolish it is to say,
"I'll remember this always."

I sit in a basement room
 looking up at snow-covered ivy
where stately pine boughs sweep down
and catch sunlight in their hands.
What falls through their fingers
sifts like dust on the snowcrust,
slides downhill, a glow brighter
than gray sky beading on the hilltop,
and rivulets trickle out to soft
thin lines by the wall below.

Winter days like these I feel underwater,
my breathing chest pushes against the air outside me,
my ears and eyes muffled in gray.
Each intention needs effort and concentration,
leads to trouble if I act without thinking,
treading those depths without a partner.

If I drift to sleep,
if I am distracted by darting schools of lightfish,
if I lose the way that up is,
I will wander forever in this fog,
swim in a kelp forest of vague intention,
unbalanced by the passing of purposeful creatures.
Struck dumb on a street corner,
I want someone to pin a note on my coat,
have someone take me somewhere.
I'm not homeless;
I just don't know where it is.

Someone loves me, but who is she?
Why have I stayed away so long that I lost her?
Must I remember before I can speak
to these strange familiar creatures?

They say if you die in your dreams
you'll die in your sleep,
but I've done it a hundred times.
The first time, I opened my mouth
and inhaled an ocean I was too deep in
to get out of.
If I do it now,
maybe I'll wake up on a beach somewhere,
or in a warm room on a bed with cool clean sheets;
and if people are kind and treat me well,
I can begin a new life,
and no one will blame me
for losing this wonderful life
I have lived until now.

NO NEW YEAR'S RESOLUTIONS

If God punishes us where we've had most fun,
        I'll die of skin cancer.
    In the meantime he takes little swipes,
        rattles a heartbeat, scratches a lung,
        sets a string of coral polyps along a moist canal,
    hints at deeper hits to come.
It's little wonder dry leaves flame,
    sky at day's end flares with burning hues,
    screams of joy coloratura as we age.
Even as I hobble out of September surf,
    I want to throw myself back,
    skip winter's coma,
    go deaf to the promise of a distant spring
    when buds and grasses must work
    harder than last year to eke out green,
    push up the nectar that sets bees abuzz,
    bloom and weaken till the raging burnout of another autumn.
Join me in this quiet crackling space:
    let's not hang on till next year, but
    throw ourselves into the sky, the inevitable chill,
    and burn what we have till no one can tell
    our ashes from the winter's snow.
No embarrassing resolutions again this year:
    we won't grit and grumble and curse
    the white world that ices our bones;
    there will be no more "Until we meet again."
We'll fire up so high,
    raise a flame that burns every place
    we ever thought of going before it goes out.
And when God comes to get us,
    He won't be able to tell us
    from wisps of mist on winter's breath.

THE CLOWN

From the bleachers we watch the tightrope family,
   and their high tension tricks hold our eyes upraised.
    Most of us can't do that,
  but all of us can perform down here—
 in garish leotard ride the bareback
horse bedecked with scarlet plumes,
be the sequined spinner on a twirling rope,
perch like a sugar plum on an elephant's head,
dance in purple gauze and violet slippers.
Maybe you would like to be the ringmaster, the pointer,
the one who tells us what to watch:
"Now in ring one the lovely Maloney sisters
sport their handmade finery
and swing from elephants' trunks.
In ring two the Pilsudski brothers
tumble with a Russian bear."
You can do that; the proof you need is me.

No matter what mistakes you make,
you can't be as foolish as I am.
Even with my makeup off, my face looks painted.
Yet silly, garish or sad, I have a place here.
Match that to your social security.
Don't let the high risk Wallendas
trick you into sticking to your seat,
open-mouthed, one hand stuck in a popcorn sack.
They will fall because they fly so high;
it's the price they pay for lifting our eyes.
But our lives can be lived as easy as laughing;
from our height the sawdust is soft as popcorn.
Join me, stand down, step into the spotlight.
Each of you can be something more than a clown.

SKINDIVER'S DREAMS

Snow-covered countryside pillows
  my ears; a great whale cloud with bulging
   belly and big smile swims crawl,
   one lobster claw pushed forward,
 the other trailing in diffuse light.

A man's thick body stands by
the roadside, his head aslant, oval
mouth moaning below upraised
arms—all the tendons, muscles
and bones unbraided to float
like fan coral. A long-headed
woman in swimfins pushes across
the surface, a shadow mottled
in sea-blue sky. Blasted brush
sways like anemones. Blackbirds
fold their wings and glide
like fish, opening and closing
their beaks in silent rhythm.

I lay my head back panting,
body fully tired from swimming.
White walls, open windows, no
ceiling except broad black sea
grape leaves sweeping purple sky.
You lie beside me, the warm
wind a damp sheet, our bodies
breathing like the waves, your dress
crocheted from red starfish
scratching my salty skin.

SWIMMING

The water rushes past my ears.
I hear the enclosed sound of myself,
like my breathing on the telephone.
I lie on my back, stretch,
and pull against the water;
my fingertips touch my thighs
and I draw them up to my breasts
and pull again, my head a prow,
my exhale the bass rhythm of a whale song.

I started this for exercise;
now I do it for therapy.
Buoyancy eases the burden of my body.
This action I have known
since before I could walk
has become another anti-gravity act
like music, sex, and laughter.

The young woman in the next lane
cuts the water like a barracuda,
wanton in her use of energy.
She has yet to hear the song pause,
know the silence when the heart
does not beat or the dance when her
tempo falters, her foot sticks to the floor.

She floats and it means nothing to her,
like the easy laughter that lifts kids
up to their ears, two lovers in a bed,
the loss of self that comes from
finding a Dali in a room of its own.

Racers convert the flat liquid to an upstream,
powering like sperm cells for a small mortal reward.
I'm beyond Freud and amniotic fluid,
shuttling between points at the ends of the pool,
vague light falling from somewhere above,
the bubbling sound of my breath,
the rhythm of my pull,
the waiting darkness beneath the wall.

AUTUMN

A filament of fishing line has stretched
  from shore to the red oak for a week now.
    Acorns drop like shot. Ducks feed, flip,
    and fling sidelong glances at flotillas of geese.
  Squirrels build fat and fur and hop fence tops.
 An old man spreads his wool coat to catch
pale warmth. My breath fogs in cool air.

I see your withering touch on the edges
of brilliant leaves, know what's beneath
the episcopal plush under the maple, wait
for the day you lie down and your breast
muffles city sounds, your kiss ices ponds,
your cool touch reaches into my entrails,
grips and lets go, but does not go away.

I have felt your palsied hand at the back
of my skull, in the blank spaces in my stare,
the slack lines along my tongue. I have known
all my life what you have planned for me,
my sister, my love, my last wife. I know why
you charm me each autumn day with
age-old turnings of your fresh face, but
still I resist your loving embrace.

THE ALUMINUM HELMET

Above the glasses tinted to screen out UVs,
    it was probably a Kangol cap covered by aluminum foil.
    I startled him out of his trance with a warm hello.
He backed off because he knows that Earth people
  who understand him want to put him away,
and he doesn't know when the aliens will show up in human form.

Transmitting radio messages through his fillings,
extraterrestrial beings are telling him to do bad things,
like "Kill the President. Only he prevents your people
from joining the family of the universe."

This one man chosen to do the work of superior beings refuses.
A shell-shocked gentle man stock still by a duck-infested pond
defends our civilization by holding to a basic value.
We must not kill individuals for any noble collective good.
And he fights the aliens by himself
because their voices never leave him alone.

Somehow he discovered that an aluminum hat muffles the orders,
but just now he was arrested by a static burst
reflected off the water's surface and up under the helmet.
Freed by my friendly gesture, he will walk quickly to his room
and bang his head against the wall until the voices stop.
But he can't hold out forever, and we had better help him.
Because the voices don't only tell him to kill presidents.
Over in the medical center a doctor experiments on babies.
A teacher abuses children. Poets poison people's minds.
Yet all the urgings of the fascists in the galaxy
can't make this lonely man kill one of us.

He won't let us mummify him in a charity mental ward.
He holds out as long as he can in fear that when he is gone
a weaker soul will become their pawn.
And on a late night drive across a high bridge
one of us will see him tight-roping the rail,
throwing the devil's last temptation back in his face:
"If you are the great power of the universe,
lift me up so that I may do your service."
And the aluminum helmet will spiral away in the wind.
He will fall,
and the world will have just one more night of unmurdered sleep.

CAPE PORPOISE

A spider hangs upside down,
 tantalized by May's first flies outside.
  The old lady grumbles into her clam roll:
  "We didn't have any spring."
 Boats moored in the estuary face the sea.
Gulls and cormorants glide by on tidal flats.
"My very favorite's swordfish," she says.
"Do you have a favorite, Helen?"

The first annoyances of summer
have returned to put the cottage into shape.
Two white-haired wrinkled faces smug in pink sweaters,
an old man in pale blue,
the back of his neck cross-hatched like netting in a lobster pot.

Strange the intimates we become in old age,
daring the spider's web
for summer's promise on spring air,
or like boats straining against the running tide,
floating worn in pale colors among commonplaces
in this safe harbor of worn rocks,
bobbing on waves made sluggish
by the first Bermuda high,
tugged between tired familiar guidepost eyes
and the cool starless eternal death seaward.

MAKING LOVE TO DEATH

"I SAT AT THE BAR MAKING LOVE TO DEATH."
—JON TAYLOR

All seduction is sham,
all interest delusion.
Death doesn't love me any more than the booze.
I can tease her, lead her on, charm her,
but Death decides.
She can keep me on the wire forever
or simply take my breath away.
If I plead with her to take me now,
she may beat the bartender to last call
before the tab is due,
but she could just as easily lock us in
and party till my body sickens
and my mind goes round the bend.
All Death's jokes have punchlines.
We wild ones gamble that Death will play along
with those who court or amuse her
because if she killed us all,
Death would die.
So I hook my heels on the bar stool,
dive into her cleavage,
and make love to her
in the absurd hope that Death will love me.

GOD'S PLAN

He handed me a pamphlet that said,
  "GOD HAS A PLAN. . . and you are in it!"
   The design was Romanesque, Moorish, Coptic,
  but if He or She exists,
 my God is Gothic, Mongol, Apache,
some fierce strategist screaming obscure orders
while I'm ass deep in some mess I never saw coming.

My God is John Madden—a loud-mouthed Sunday maniac
commanding me to battle according to a logical weekly plan
obscured by the dirt, panic and mayhem around me.

. . .or maybe She is a terrible wife-mother combination
urging me to love and keep my fly zipped, cuddle yet be strong,
show the non-threatening vulnerability of Alan Alda
in the invincible stride of Arnold Schwartzenegger

. . .or maybe God is a benign rapmaster DJ
merely spinning the tune we dance to,
scratching segments and replaying tiny parts for deja vu
just to mess with the idea we are making progress.

Creation isn't complete until Armageddon.
The celestial city planner is always catching up
to conditions set in motion for His or Her amusement,
so the only salvation we have is to act in that image
and dance across the chaos till the time bell rings.

THE BLUE JAY

He's bigger than full grown,
  an aging tackle with bull neck and wide shoulders,
   but with a twitch that's his own.
They all have that head snap, the quick hop,
  but this one's got a spastic tic that puts him off balance.
 He can't handle the fence top
with the usual blue jay's aplomb.
A croak haunts his call when
he spreads himself and settles in hot grass,
cleaner than any Audubon illustration,
his tail bars static and vibrant as pieces of sea spray on the dull lawn,
catching as much sun as he can.
He's too far gone,
grown beyond his span,
needing more light than day can give him.
Some morning soon too late he'll shout.
The landlord's labs will have him in their jaws,
toss him about, and thick cerulean shards
will swirl like pieces of sky falling in the yards.

FALLING WALLENDAS

Behold a Wallenda stopped at mid-line;
   years of discipline hold him up,
     but he's lost the desire to cross
   and the crowd can't help him.
  If it were AJ at Indy,
 the gas would run out,
the machinery stop,
and the crew lift him out of the car.
But what can we do when the mind is gone,
the body goes on,
and we're too weak to jump,
too stubborn to let go?

I think of Eddie Balchowsky,
a concert pianist who lost an arm on the Ebro.
He scattered body parts and brain cells in his past
like some joyous Johnny Appleseed of common sense
who finally couldn't bang himself sane
and scraped together transit fare
to step in front of the train,
a Wallenda giving up his grip on the wire,
shivering off the balance that made him a household name,
dropping like a precious stone
set in the golden ring of memory.

BEARER DONATES BODY TO NATURE

The gulf breathes evenly at my side;
  wind in the saw grass sounds the sigh
  of her hair as she turns. North on Mobile Bay
  lightning flashes. Cannonades alternate
from west to east, a romantic lightshow
  till awkward bright bolts strike.
A great neon dogleg illuminates the road
and twitches twice. Tug boats, electric
generators, and barges rumble below
the storm like the purr in her cat's chest
reverberating in my love's breast.

All sensation ends in death;
  it lurks beneath the regular breath.
Delicious pathways crackle and streak
across cloudtops like trace elements
in brain fluid alive with remembered fire,
  like the static snap in her hair.
  In the pineland of memory I sit
  and savor songs, photos in hand,
  tasting her in the salty air—
brief chorus and soft pillars of light
to guide and chase me into the night.

In daylight earth's respiration
  continues its maternal motion,
fruitful parent to all I have enjoyed.
In clean spring air birds send high
frequency mating calls. I have planned
  this forever: desolate stretch
  of Gulf Coast, shotgun, bearable
  cancer unbearable now. I wade
  out, suck the barrel, trigger one sear-
ing bolt of mechanical fire flung long
to kill the feeling and stop the song.